New Zealand Travel Guide

The Ultimate Guide to Discover the Magic of Kiwi Land and Māori Culture | Explore the Captivating Landscapes that Inspired Writers and Adventures

ARIKI SINGH

Table of Contents

Introduction

Greetings from the kingdom of the long white cloud, where lush green mountains meet glistening blue waterways and spectacular views await you around every bend. From the golden beaches of the Bay of Islands to the snow-capped summits of the Southern Alps, New Zealand is a place of contrasts and natural wonders. And our 2023 New Zealand Travel Guide is the best resource for discovering this amazing nation.

Our guide includes everything you need, whether you're an adventure seeker hoping to bungee jump in Queenstown or a foodie eager to try the regional fare. From hiking through old woods to basking in hot springs under the stars, we've combed the entire nation to bring you the best experiences.

However, our guide is more than just a rundown of things to do and see. We'll also introduce you to the people that make New Zealand unique, from the welcoming locals to the guardians of the Maori culture. You'll find undiscovered attractions that only locals are aware of and learn insider strategies for making the most of your trip in this fascinating nation.

Our New Zealand Travel Guide 2023 is the ideal travel companion, so whether you're organizing a once-in-a-lifetime vacation or are an experienced traveler looking for your next adventure, it is the book you need. Don't just take our word for it; come along with us as we explore one of the world's most stunning and fascinating nations.

Chapter 1:
Welcome to New Zealand

The two main islands in the magnificent country of New Zealand, which is made up of innumerable smaller islands and is located in the southwest Pacific Ocean, are the South Island and the North Island. The country is well known for its stunning natural surroundings, unique wildlife, and rich cultural legacy.

Approximately 1,500 kilometers east of Australia are the two main islands of New Zealand, the North Island, and the South Island. The diversified landscape of the country includes rough mountains, lush forests, sandy beaches, and undulating hills. Although the North Island is more populated and has a milder, more temperate climate than the South Island, the South Island is recognized for its alpine climate and magnificent beauty, particularly the Southern Alps Mountain range.

New Zealand experiences mild temperatures and a yearly average rainfall that is quite high. The weather can be highly unpredictable, with four distinct seasons and the possibility of severe weather events like cyclones, floods, and droughts.

New Zealand's colonial past with Europe and its indigenous Maori people has significantly impacted the country's history and culture. The Maori have a strong sense of cultural identity based on their ties to the land and their use of age-old techniques like weaving, carving, and performing arts.

The British colonized New Zealand in the 19th century, which significantly influenced the nation's history and culture. The population of New Zealand is varied now, with members descended from European, Maori, Pacific Island, and Asian ancestry.Fun Information About New Zealand:

- ❖ The Kakapo, the only flightless parrot in the world, can be found only in New Zealand.
- ❖ Taumatawhakatangihangakoauauotamateaturipukak apikimaungahoronukupokaiwhenuakitanatahu, a hill in the Hawke's Bay region, has the nation's longest place name in the entire world.
- ❖ New Zealand was the first country to grant women the right to vote in 1893.
- ❖ There are roughly six sheep for every person in the nation, which has more sheep than humans.

Practical Information for Travelers

Consider a few things if you are considering visiting New Zealand. First, you must disclose any food, plant, or animal products while entering the country due to the strong biosecurity rules to protect the nation's distinctive flora and animals. Second, there is a wide variety of lodging available in New Zealand, including hotels, motels, hostels, and campgrounds. The nation is renowned for its outstanding network of Department of Conservation (DOC) campgrounds, which are dispersed throughout some of the nation's most stunning and inaccessible regions.

Finally, New Zealand has a vast system of hiking trails, or "+tramping," as they are called there. The routes here can take you from a pleasant stroll in the park to a challenging hike into the woods, so choose your adventure wisely. New Zealand is a lovely and distinctive country with plenty to offer every kind of traveler, from breathtaking natural scenery and a rich cultural legacy to challenging outdoor activities and hospitable residents.

Chapter 2:
Planning Your Trip

When organizing your trip to New Zealand, there are a few important factors to consider, such as the need for a visa and immigration procedures, travel arrangements, lodging, and financial planning.

Visa and immigration requirements: Most of tourists to New Zealand require a visa to enter the nation, though the requirements differ based on your nationality and the planned length of your stay. On the New Zealand immigration website, you can look up the visa requirements for your nation.

How to get to New Zealand: Long-distance travelers have a few options for getting to New Zealand, including flying or taking a cruise ship. Sydney, Melbourne, Los Angeles, and Hong Kong are just a few of the main places in the world from which there are direct flights to New Zealand.

Transportation options within the country: Once in New Zealand, you can choose various transportation alternatives, including renting a car, taking a bus or coach, or using the public transportation system in bigger cities. Although some regions of the country can be remote and difficult to get to, New Zealand has a well-developed transportation network and is generally easy to get around.

Where to stay: Many different types of lodging are available in New Zealand, including hotels, motels, bed and breakfasts, vacation parks, and rental homes. Your preferences will determine whether you stay in a city or a more rural area.

Budgeting and finances: The New Zealand dollar (NZD) is the local currency. The cost of living in New Zealand varies depending on where you live and what you do, although it is generally more expensive than in other countries. Planning your trip's budget and having a rough idea of how much money you'll need to pay for your expenses are good selections. Credit cards are commonly accepted in New Zealand, and ATMs can be found in most towns and cities.

Visa And Immigration Requirements

Most visitors to New Zealand require a visa to enter the country, though the requirements vary depending on your nationality and the length of your stay.

You can stay in New Zealand for up to six months without a visa if you have a current passport, a return ticket, or a ticket to another country. Australia, Canada, the United States, and most of Europe do not require visas.

If you are a national of a country that does not grant visa waivers or want to stay in New Zealand for more than six months, you must apply for a visa before your trip. Visitors can enter New Zealand on several visas, including tourist, working holiday, and student visas.

To be considered for a visa, you must submit an online application form with supporting evidence, such as a current passport, proof of finances, and a return or onward ticket. You may also be required to provide a police clearance certificate and proof of health insurance.

Applying for your visa well in advance ensures you have all you need to visit New Zealand. More information regarding visa and immigration requirements can be found on the New Zealand immigration website.

How To Get to New Zealand

There are numerous ways to get to New Zealand, depending on your origin.

Flying is the most frequent way to arrive in New Zealand. Direct flights to New Zealand are available from many major cities worldwide, including Sydney, Melbourne, Los Angeles, and Hong Kong. Connecting flights are also available from many other places, albeit these may include layovers and lengthier journey times.

You can find flights to New Zealand through a travel agent or online booking platform. Prices might vary greatly based on the time of year, the route, and how long in advance you book, so shop around and compare prices. Another option for getting to New Zealand is by taking a cruise ship. New Zealand is a popular port of call for many cruise companies, and many itineraries include the country. This can be a good option if you're interested in visiting several regional destinations and want a more leisurely way to travel. Once you arrive in New Zealand, you'll most likely land at one of the country's main airports, which are located in the major cities of Auckland, Wellington, and Christchurch. From there, you can travel to your destination by rental car, public transportation, or shuttle bus.

Where to Stay

There are many types of lodging available in New Zealand, including hotels, motels, bed & breakfasts, vacation parks, and rental homes, to accommodate a variety of budgets and preferences.

Hotels and motels are generally accessible in major cities and villages, including affordable and upscale choices. If you want a more conventional lodging with all the amenities you would anticipate, such as a private bathroom, room service, and a reception desk, hotels and motels are a wonderful choice.

Bed and breakfasts (B&Bs) are a more private and cozy lodging typically found in a private home or guesthouse. If you want a more regional and genuine experience, B&Bs are a good choice, and they frequently include a home-cooked breakfast as part of the package.

Holiday parks are a well-liked form of lodging in New Zealand, particularly for tourists on a budget or those on a family vacation. Holiday parks offer a variety of lodging alternatives, from camping and caravan sites to cottages and flats, and are frequently situated in picturesque areas.

Rental properties, another choice for lodging in New Zealand is apartments or vacation houses. Rental properties can offer more space and privacy than other types of accommodation and can be a good option if you're traveling with a group or planning to stay in one place for an extended period.

Overall, New Zealand has many hotel options, so you should be able to find something to suit your interests and budget. It's a good idea to book hotel reservations beforehand, especially if you're visiting a popular tourist site or during peak season. Money and Budgeting

The New Zealand dollar is used as money there (NZD). It's a smart idea to budget your vacation in advance and have a rough idea of how much cash you'll need to cover your expenses, including housing, transportation, meals, and activities. New Zealand's cost of living might vary based on where you are and what you are doing, but overall, it is a more expensive country than some other places to visit. Most visitors to New Zealand spend most of their vacation budget on hotels and transportation, which can vary widely in price based on personal preferences.

Food and drink in New Zealand can also be costly, especially in popular tourist destinations and big cities. Consider self-catering or eating at neighborhood cafes and restaurants rather than more expensive tourist places. It's a good idea to shop around and compare prices.

Credit cards are accepted frequently in New Zealand, and ATMs can be found in most towns and cities. Additionally, having cash on hand is a smart idea, especially if you plan to visit more remote or rural areas.

To get the most of your trip to New Zealand, it's critical to plan ahead and be aware of your budget. Additionally, it's a good idea to plan for some budget flexibility to cover unforeseen costs or take advantage of last-minute chances.

Chapter 3:
Essential Information for the Traveler

Important phone numbers for Emergency Services (police, fire, ambulance)- **111**

Local Operator- **010**

International Operator- **0170**

New Zealand Directory Assistance- **018**

International Directory- **0172**

New Zealand offers a variety of lodging options, from hostels to hotels of different kinds. Booking as far in advance as possible, preferably at least two days, is advised. If you are traveling, especially during the peak travel season (December to February) or during a public holiday or a school break always confirm your hotel reservations. Although Palmerston North, Hamilton, Queenstown, and Dunedin all receive some flights from Australia, Auckland, Christchurch, and

Wellington are the main airports. New Zealand's legal drinking age is 18. Anyone who seems to be under 25 must show identification to purchase alcohol. Banks are open for business from Monday through Friday during these times (except for federal holidays). All major credit cards can be used at ATMs found around New Zealand.

The business infrastructure, including the telecommunications and transportation networks, is top-notch. Locating business services won't be difficult. Some hotels have their own secretarial staff. More than 25% of the population of New Zealand lives in Auckland on the North Island. Wellington, the nation's capital, is located south of North Island. The largest city in the South Island is called Christchurch.

Except for Northland, where it is subtropical, the climate is temperate. The usual summer temperature is from 20 to 30 degrees Celsius, while the winter ranges from 10-15 degrees Celsius. The seasons in New Zealand run counterclockwise to those in the Northern Hemisphere. Outside of the alpine regions, no temperatures are below freezing.

Since the weather might change suddenly, it's smart to always have a sweater on hand if you need to layer up. If you plan on traveling during the winter, bring some warm clothes and an umbrella. There are 10 cent, 20 cent, 50 cent, $1, $2, $5, $10, $20, $50, and $100 denominations of the New Zealand dollar (NZ$).

Traveler checks and major credit cards are accepted in hotels, banks, and retail establishments. Most banks are members of Cirus or Plus. Airfare may exclude departure tax. A fee of $22 to $25 must be paid by all adults (12 and older) leaving New Zealand (except at Christchurch and Auckland Airports). You can pay for this at the airport with cash or a credit card.

Regional airports have the right to charge a domestic departure fee. Make sure the building offers access for people with disabilities before making a reservation because it is required by law. You should, if necessary, investigate obtaining a parking discount using a mobility card or medical certificate. You may find Enable New Zealand at www.weka.net.nz.

If you plan on driving while in New Zealand, you must bring your valid driver's license from your home country or get international driving permission. In addition to downtown duty-free shops that will ship items to airports, you can purchase duty-free goods in airport shops when you arrive and depart. Electricity at 230/240 volts is accessible in New Zealand (50 hertz).

For the use of electric shavers, most hotels have 110-volt, 20-watt a/c plugs. An adaptor is needed for most other devices. Only flat 2-3-pin plugs are accepted in power outlets. You can connect your laptop to a computer socket using an RJ 45-type connector and an adaptor with a flat 2–3-point plug to connect the power supply.

The moniker "clean and green" given to Environment New Zealand is deserving. Utilizing the well-known sustainable travel and tourism brand Green Globe New Zealand, more and more tourism-related enterprises.

New Zealanders typically have a friendly, courteous, and inviting attitude toward visitors. In New Zealand, no formalized system of classes is in force.

Chapter 4:
When to Visit New Zealand

It could not be easy to pick the ideal time of year to visit New Zealand. In New Zealand, there are four seasons, each with distinct advantages and disadvantages for the travel industry. We'll review each season's advantages and disadvantages to help you decide when it's best to travel to New Zealand. New Zealand has four unique seasons, each attracting a different type of tourist. There are many different types of flowering in the spring, festivities, outdoor activities, adrenaline-pumping sports in the summer, vivid foliage in the fall, and fluffy snow for a fantastic ski season in the winter. The seasons are completely different from those in the north due to the location in the southern hemisphere. As a result, while Americans are shoveling snow and setting up their Christmas decorations, people in New Zealand are soaking up the sun in the hottest months of the year.

New Zealanders love the time of year when the leaves change color as we watch the flowers bloom. While we are gathering leaves and getting ready for another winter, New Zealanders are enjoying spring in all its splendor during the harshest months of the year in the northern hemisphere.

This makes New Zealand the ideal winter getaway for people in the northern hemisphere because you can exchange your bulky coats and boots for sunlight and flip-flops (or jandals, as the Kiwis refer to them!)

The best time to visit New Zealand is frequently during the summer, from January to March when the days are long and bright, and the temperatures are warmer.

Your attitude, though, can vary based on what you expect to achieve from your trip.

The greatest time to visit New Zealand is in the spring when the weather is mild (perfect for trekking!), with fewer visitors. Your attitude, though, can vary based on what you expect to achieve from your trip.

(October, November, September)

If you want to take advantage of the comfortable temperatures, lengthy daylight hours, and beach days, summer is the best time to visit New Zealand. **(November, December, and February)**

Autumn is the ideal time to visit New Zealand if you want to avoid enormous crowds while still having enough daylight and comfortable temperatures to enjoy a variety of outdoor activities. **(April, May, March)**

Whether you want to go skiing or are on a tight budget, winter is the best time to visit New Zealand because it offers the highest discounts and the fewest tourists. However, you must also be at ease with dropping temperatures, shorter days, and the seasonal closure of many of activities.

(July, August, and June)

We prefer to visit New Zealand around November or December, which are the months between spring and summer, but more on that in a moment. It turns out that this is one of those questions that genuinely has no right solution. There are benefits and drawbacks to each season. But there's no need to panic. To help you choose the best time of year for you, we'll go over the benefits and drawbacks of visiting New Zealand during each season.

Start by answering the following questions:

- ❖ Do you detest being cold?
- ❖ Do you find crowds to be stressful?
- ❖ Do you enjoy winter sports like snowboarding and skiing?
- ❖ Or while you're outside, do you prefer cycling, kayaking, or hiking?
- ❖ Do you appreciate extreme sports like whitewater rafting?
- ❖ Bright fall foliage or fresh spring blossoms — which would you like to see?

By considering your answers to these questions, you may begin choosing the best time to visit New Zealand.

New Zealand comprises roughly 600 islands in the southwest Pacific Ocean. New Zealand is an extremely small nation, with its two main islands, North Island and South Island, about 1,600 kilometers (1,600 miles) apart.

Since the North and South Islands are New Zealand's largest and most populous, they will be our primary areas of exploration. Sand beaches, mountain ranges, fjord-like sounds, rolling green hills, glacial lakes, and valleys with vineyards are just a few examples of the islands' diverse topography.

Weather in New Zealand

It's crucial to remember that such differences in the terrain correspond to specific temperatures and weather patterns. Since New Zealand has no true tropical regions, its climate can be described as highly diverse, ranging from desert to subtropical.

Be prepared because it's possible to experience all four seasons in one day in New Zealand.

Even though New Zealand's weather can be a little unpredictable, it is often warm, with an average regional difference between winter and summer temperatures of only about 10°C.

No area of the country experiences frequent temperature fluctuations between 86°F/30°C and 32°F/0°C. Due to the moderate temperature range and lack of extremes, tropical storms do not regularly affect New Zealand.

However, it does experience a LOT of earthquakes because of its position on two important tectonic plates.

Facts about New Zealand's seasons and weather:

❖ In New Zealand, January through February are the warmest months.

- ❖ In New Zealand, July is the coldest to the chilliest month.
- ❖ The three wettest months in New Zealand are March, December, and July (in Auckland, Wellington, and Christchurch) (in Central Otago)
- ❖ In New Zealand, January is the busiest month. The driest months are February and July (in Auckland, Wellington, and Christchurch); (Queenstown).
- ❖ May is the least crowded month in New Zealand.

Which type of weather can I expect in New Zealand?

This is a challenging question to answer because the answer largely relies on the region of the country you want to visit.

The question "What is the temperature in Europe in January?" comes to mind.

The climate in Scotland will be very different from that in Barcelona. Or "How warm is it in the United States in April? The reaction in Seattle will be very different from that in Miami. For instance, the Bay of Islands in Northland enjoys a subtropical climate, yet the mountain settlements on the southernmost end of the South Island might periodically suffer far cooler and more extreme weather.

Despite major geographical variances, the New Zealand travel guide lists the following as the normal daily temperatures:

Spring:

- ❖ October, September, and November
- ❖ 61 – 66°F (16 – 19°C)

Summer:

- ❖ January, February, and December
- ❖ 68 – 77°F (20 – 25°C)

Autumn:

- ❖ April, May, and March
- ❖ 62 – 70°F (17 – 21°C)

Winter:

- ❖ July, August, and June
- ❖ 53 – 61°F (12 – 16°C)

You can find the average temperatures for each region here, which might help you plan your itinerary by letting you know what to expect in each location.

The New Zealand Summer

The biggest travel season in New Zealand is the summer when temperatures are at their greatest and crowds are at their densest. Many New Zealanders take time off work during the school breaks, and many establishments — including restaurants and shops — might be closed for weeks. Booking in advance is recommended if you plan to visit New Zealand now, as hotels may be full due to the high number of tourists.

The summer months in brief:

Summer technically begins in December, along with, of course, holiday breaks. This month is the best time to see penguins in the south.

Since most people take vacations in January, there won't be as many restaurants and cafés open during that period. In addition, hotel rates will be at their peak.

The best time to visit the beach in New Zealand is February, the hottest month of the year. Fewer establishments will close their doors by this time because the locals will have returned to work. New Zealand vacation spots for the summer

- ❖ Waitomo Glowworm Caves are open from November to April (the caves get too cold in the winter)
- ❖ Beaches at Coromandel Peninsula Beaches and outdoor activities may be available at Abel Tasman National Park. The Otago Peninsula and Dunedin are great places to watch penguins.
- ❖ at Stewart Island in December
- ❖ The best months to visit Waiheke Island are February or March.

Best summer activities in New Zealand

- ❖ explore the beach.
- ❖ observing southern penguins
- ❖ hiking, outdoor pursuits, and kayaking
- ❖ View some of the best campgrounds in New Zealand.
- ❖ the January Parihaka Peace Festival

- ❖ The World Buskers' Festival is hosted in Christchurch (January) (January)
- ❖ Auckland's Laneway Festival (January)
- ❖ Check out the New Zealand Sevens rugby competition (January)

The ideal season to travel to New Zealand is summer if...

- ❖ You're not actually against crowds.
- ❖ You want for sunny skies and mild temperatures.
- ❖ You want to go to the beach.
- ❖ Reservations can be made well in advance.
- ❖ What to bring for a summer vacation to New Zealand:
- ❖ pest prevention (solids are the way to go because sandflies really suck)
- ❖ Wear a thin jacket or fleece for sports.
- ❖ a raincoat
- ❖ Strong walking or hiking sandals (we prefer Chacos to hiking boots because they're lighter and more practical in damp weather).
- ❖ reef-friendly sunscreen
- ❖ Swimsuits

New Zealand, autumn

Fall is the best season for trekking since the temperature is just beginning to cool off but the sun is still shining for long, crisp days.

The busiest time of year for tourists is passed, people have returned to work, and the trails are less crowded. New Zealand, the leaves change color with the seasons, going from green to brilliant orange, yellow, and scarlet hues.

Months of autumn in a nutshell:

Most days are still sunny and pleasant, even though spring officially ends in March. This "shoulder season" month is ideal for seeing popular sights without the hassle of crowds. New Zealand's spectacular autumn foliage is at its best in April. After the Easter holiday, tourism drops significantly, making finding a place to stay easier. By May, New Zealand's temperatures will have dropped significantly, necessitating thermal underwear and other layers. Kayak says May is also the most cost-effective time to fly from the United States to New Zealand. The best places in New Zealand to visit in the fall

- ❖ March brings Blenheim and the Marlborough wine region.
- ❖ Although the autumn is the driest season, the grapes are in full bloom in the Central Otago wine region.
- ❖ April is when the leaves change in Hawkes Bay.
- ❖ the greater Mackenzie Country and Lake Tekapo's April leaf-turning season.
- ❖ Area of Southern Alpine April hiking on an island
- ❖ In the fall or winter, Auckland (to escape the spring or summer crowds)

The best things to do in New Zealand in the fall

- ❖ Visit some of the top wineries in New Zealand.

- ❖ seeing and taking pictures of fall foliage
- ❖ Go outside and engage in one of New Zealand's best adventures.
- ❖ Auckland's Pasifika Cultural Festival
- ❖ March brings the Waikato Balloons Over Hamilton Festival.
- ❖ Wanaka's Festival of Color (April)
- ❖ The Royal Easter Show in Auckland (April)
- ❖ Hamilton's Great New Zealand Food Show (May)

The best time to visit New Zealand is in the fall.

- ❖ To engage in outside activities, you want the weather to be agreeable.
- ❖ You want to see (and take pictures of!) the changing leaves.
- ❖ You prefer to avoid crowded places.
- ❖ You relish the clean, crisp air.
- ❖ You want to visit vineyards because you enjoy tasting wine.

What to pack for a trip to New Zealand in the fall:

- ❖ Wind- and rain-resistant jacket
- ❖ A shawl
- ❖ Thermal coverings
- ❖ Cozy socks
- ❖ hiking or walking boots

New Zealand, winter

Snow falls during the winter. Snowbirds from the Northern Hemisphere seeking "off-season" skiing arrive all through the ski season.

During this season, especially in the high country, roads may be a little treacherous. However, there is very little snow in the lowlands, and it becomes quite warm in the valleys.

The North Island frequently experiences more winters precipitation than the South Island. In Auckland and Queenstown, the winter is the wettest and driest time of year.

Overview of the winter months:

The ski season in New Zealand officially begins in June. Ski resorts welcome visitors as the first snow in the Alps falls. In June, the indigenous Mori people celebrate Matariki, their New Year.

July and August often have the best snow conditions for skiing. Except for ski resorts, this is New Zealand's off-season, when prices and availability are at their lowest.

Best locations to visit in New Zealand during the winter

- ❖ Tongariro National Park throughout the winter (better to avoid the busy months of November to April).
- ❖ South Island's Pancake Rocks, which are amazing all year long but are especially fun in the winter.
- ❖ Franz Josef Glacier in Glacier Country in the winter (avoid visiting during the summer months!

Fiordland experiences crisp, sunny days in winter, but be ready for the chill!

Best winter activities in New Zealand

- ❖ Skiing and snowboarding
- ❖ Music, snow sports, and entertainment during the Queenstown Winter Festival (Jun/Jul)
- ❖ Midwinter Carnival in Dunedin (June)
- ❖ The Festival of Lights in Lyttelton (June)
- ❖ The Chocolate Carnival in Dunedin (July)
- ❖ An international film festival is held in New Zealand (July)

The month of Restaurants in Auckland (August)

- ❖ Fashion Week in New Zealand (August): Wellington on a Visa Plate (August)

The best ski resorts in New Zealand

In New Zealand, the ski season normally lasts from June through the first week of October.

- ❖ Ruapehu and Taranaki are the North Island's two primary ski areas.
- ❖ The South Island's three largest ski areas are in Wanaka, Otago, and Canterbury.

Winter is the best time to visit New Zealand.

- ❖ It doesn't bother you if it becomes cold.

29

- You want to snowboard or go skiing.
- Avoid being in a mob of people.
- You should go on your trip off-peak to save money.

What to bring with you to New Zealand for winter

- Layers, such as a layered jacket, gloves, and a hat
- Cozy, comfy footwear
- Woolen socks
- Sunglasses (keep in mind that the sharp snow reflection might be!).
- A beanie or winter hat
- Ski equipment (if needed)

New Zealand, springtime

In New Zealand, hiking and other outdoor activities become popular when springtime fully blooms. As the temperature warms, the flora comes to life. Remember to pack a windbreaker because spring is New Zealand's windiest season! The mountains still have snow on their summits, and the sight is beautiful. Whitewater rafting is at its peak now since the rivers are raging and the snow on the mountains is melting.

Overview of the spring months:

The weather in September may be a little unpredictable and erratic. Most ski areas are still open in September, even though spring is only beginning in the lowlands. In October, the ski season comes to an end. But do not worry — the nicest spring weather is in this month.

In New Zealand, November is sometimes considered the start of summer. The temperature is warming, and tourism is on the rise. Best locations to visit in New Zealand in spring

Wellington - October normally has the finest weather, so avoid going during September when it rains the most.

- ❖ Hawkes Bay: trees in bloom
- ❖ When the gardens and parks are in flower in the spring, Christchurch, frequently referred to as "the garden city," is the best time to visit.
- ❖ Te Whakarewarewa Geothermal Valley in Rotorua

The best springtime activities in New Zealand

- ❖ Annual Alexandra Cherry Festival and Rhododendron Festival in Taranaki Garden (North Island) (September)
- ❖ The festival of cherry blossoms in Nelson (September)
- ❖ Festival of the Arts in Auckland (October)
- ❖ Hawkes Bay Festival of the Arts (October)
- ❖ Diwali celebrations are held in Aukland and Wellington (October)

The best time to visit New Zealand is in the spring.

- ❖ It should be warm (not too cold or too hot)
- ❖ You appreciate blooming flowers and don't mind the erratic weather.

What to bring with you to New Zealand for spring

- ❖ A pair of relaxed walking shoes
- ❖ Rain boots
- ❖ Cozy outerwear
- ❖ A shawl

Chapter 5:
How to Get Here, Travel and Transport

Although traveling to New Zealand is challenging, the effort is well worth it. More direct flights are available, but because they may be more expensive, most travelers choose to make one or two stops. A trip to this part of the world is more than possible with some forethought and a "think outside the box" attitude. The best choice is to fly to Australia and then take a brief flight between Australia and New Zealand if your destination is in Europe or somewhere else farther away. It's nice that so many airlines provide stops in important cities like Singapore and Kuala Lumpur while flying from Europe. Before arriving at your destination, make a little stopover in one of these wonderful nations. The website Skyscanner (www.skyscanner.com) is a fantastic resource for finding flights. This online price comparison site gives you the greatest deal by considering all the flights, prices, and airlines in your search parameters.

Just keep in mind that the greatest deal can involve three layovers and an eight-hour gap between flights. Before making a reservation, double check all the information to make sure you have allotted enough time to travel from one flight to another. Also, don't forget to bring a nice book!

You might go directly to a travel agent if you still need help finding flights that suit you. They can give you the finest advice on the airlines that offer routes to the location you're looking for. Watch for airline deals in January; you can grab a great fare if you're lucky. Flying within New Zealand

Domestic flights inside New Zealand can be pricey; therefore, booking ahead of time is generally recommended. Because New Zealand has only two airlines, there isn't much competition to keep fares down.

Air New Zealand, the country's largest domestic airline, connects the larger cities with the smaller towns. This company offers four separate fare categories, allowing you to pay for your requirements. Traveling outside large cities is substantially more expensive (a one-way ticket from Auckland to Hawkes Bay, for example, costs around NZD 100). Jetstar is a no-frills, low-cost airline that makes travel between major cities cheaper. However, flights in the early morning or late at night are routinely arranged.

If you need baggage, always double-check your ticket to ensure it is included, as it is only sometimes guaranteed. Avoid arriving late at the airport; Jetstar is notorious for sticking to stringent check-in schedules. The planes are comfortable and fast and provide stunning aerial views of New Zealand.

Why not drive instead?

The simplest method of transportation is by far renting a car. Every airport has automobile rental agencies with various vehicles for different price ranges. Budget, Avis, Thrifty, and

Hertz are the four most common car rental companies. Each day's cost typically ranges from $30 to $100 based on some variables. It's important to remember to ask when picking up your rental car because some companies won't let you take it on the ferry between the North and South Islands. If you intend to stay for an extended period, purchasing a vehicle is a viable option. This is typically less expensive than renting a car for an extended period. This requires more thought than the other options because you want to guarantee that the car you buy is mechanically sound. The last thing you want is a breakdown at three a.m. on a deserted road (trust me, I've been there).

On weekends, there are numerous vehicle markets in the larger cities. Turners Car Auctions (www.turners.co.nz), where you can bid on automobiles through an auctioneer, and TradeMe (www.trademe.co.nz), where you can buy privately from vendors, are additional options.

Taxis

In the major city areas, taxis are simple to find, and there are taxi ranks at all the major airports, train stations, and bus terminals. Uber (www.uber.com) taxis were early adopters in the nation's major cities. Using this app, you may quickly find a taxi, private automobile, or ride-sharing service.

Catch a Bus

Another simple (and affordable) method of getting around New Zealand is by bus. You can physically travel from the top of the North Island to the bottom of the South Island. There are primarily two businesses that provide this service. The first one is the Naked Bus, which frequently offers discounted prices starting at just $1 (www.nakedbus.com). The bigger of the two businesses, Intercity, is the alternative.

Both regular bus services and sightseeing services are provided. Despite having more bus routes and departure times than the Naked Bus, they are the most expensive of the two.

A ticket will cost roughly $40, depending on your destination. There are also express city-to-city bus services offered by www.manabus.com on the North Island. With the hop-on, hop-off backpacker bus excursion known as Kiwi Experience (www.kiwiexperience.com), you may travel, see the sights, and spend the night in the nicest hostels. The Connect Bus (www.connectabus.com) links Queenstown with Wanaka and Arrowtown in the South Island. The quality of bus service varies between places, but most cities and towns offer some form of bus service. Each city has a unique travel card that may be topped off with cash or a credit card to be used on buses. Britomart Transport Station in Auckland's Central Business District is the departure point for numerous excursions, trains, and buses that frequently go to other parts of the nation (CBD).

TIP: Purchase the AT Hop card for trains and buses in Auckland to save up to 20%

Trains

The train system in Auckland isn't always reliable. Although regular trains do operate, delays are frequently experienced. We recommend allowing an additional fifteen minutes when using the train. The station personnel are kind and personable and will give you whatever information you require. In New Zealand, there are three beautiful passenger rail routes. This is a simple and leisurely method to travel the nation, allowing you to sit back and take it all in. On the Northern Explorer, you will go through Tongariro National Park, which features three magnificent volcanic ranges.

Ruapehu, Tongariro, and Ngauruhoe. Extremes can be found there, including pastures covered in snow, old lava flows, and lush beech forests.

You can effortlessly travel in only eleven hours from Auckland to Wellington. Get on the Coastal Pacific train, which will take you across the beautiful South Island Pacific coastline and ride it southbound.

Travel down the Pacific Coast, where on one side, you are greeted by the roaring ocean and on the other by mountains covered in dense vegetation.

You'll finish the journey in about five and a half hours. Why not spend a few hours at the renowned Kaikoura on the way? Be warned that this train service only operates from the end of September to the beginning of May.

Do you like mountains covered with snow? Try the TranzAlpine train, which travels in about four and a half hours between Christchurch and Greymouth. Cross the Waimakariri River's spectacular gorges through the farmlands of the Canterbury Plains. Continue to the Southern Alps, where there are several photo opportunities that you must see to believe. Enter Greymouth after one final bend through a beech grove and get ready to embark on an exciting new journey.

Biking

Another excellent choice is biking, and visitors to our trails come from all over the world. The topography is varied, but the plains' relatively flat ground makes it ideal for beginning bikers. In some areas, the terrain is mountainous, making movement around difficult. Remember that always wearing a helmet and a high-visibility jacket at night in New Zealand is required. Please remember that riding on the pavement will result in a few furious looks.

In the major towns and popular tourist destinations, you can rent bikes by the hour or the day, and they will always come equipped with everything you need. It's an excellent method to discover a place.

The Ferry

What is the most efficient way to travel between islands? Flying is, of course, a possibility. The alternative way is to take the ferry from Wellington across the Cook Strait to Picton (or vice versa). Two ferry companies, Interislander (www.interislander.co.nz) and Bluebridge (www.bluebridge.co.nz), will take you from one side to the other throughout this three-hour trip. Interislander has up to eleven daily sailings, while Bluebridge has four. Both ferries will transport both vehicles and people. Although reservations are recommended, there are frequently places available for walk-ins.

Chapter 6:
New Zealand Sample Itineraries

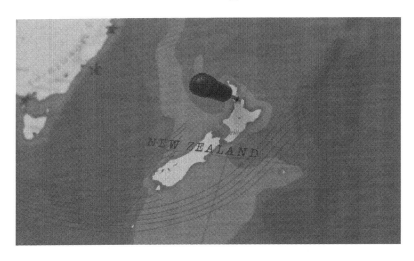

North Island Itinerary for 1 to 2 Days

It is recommended to stay at least two days if you are visiting the North Island.

First Day: Go to Taupo and check out the Tongariro Crossing for a fantastic day-long hike on your first day there. At Taupo, you will pass three volcanoes: Ngauruhoe, Ruapehu, and Tongariro. You can swim or dive with dolphins in the afternoon at Paihia, a little seaside village, after a strenuous day of hiking.

Second Day: On your second day, you can visit the Bay of Islands, which is close to Paihia. Go for a dip in the tranquil Coromandel Peninsula before visiting Rotorua. Coromandel's tourist attractions are only a one-and-a-half-hour journey from the Thames.

South Island Itinerary for 1 to 3 Days

It is advised to stay at least three days if you are visiting the South Island.

First Day: Engage in low-key outdoor activities to start the day. Once you arrive in Picton, board a bus to Nelson and relax in the waterfront city's shopping, wine tasting, and other attractions. Take some time to relax and save energy for your second and third days on the South Island because it's a lengthy trip.

Second Day: You can visit the World of Wearable Art & Classic Cars Museum on your second day. If you enjoy ice sports and exciting activities, you can brave the inclement weather and descend the steep West Coast. You may see the Pancake Rocks nearby, composed of pancake-like limestone formations.

Third Day: On the third day, you can visit Westland Tai Poutini National Park to observe the Franz Josef Glacier. You can hike, trek, or stroll on the glaciers here. The flow rates are at least ten times faster than those of most glaciers. Since there are many things to do in the glaciers, you could easily spend a whole day there.

Two-island Trip for 14 to 15 days

Despite its tiny size, New Zealand is one of the world's most geographically diverse tourist destinations. One reason is that it continuously changes, so seeing it from the road is better. Regular New Zealand travelers recommend that first-time visitors spend time exploring both the North and South Islands. Both islands may be visited in two or three weeks, but you will fall in love with New Zealand if you stay longer.

North Island

Auckland. Start by visiting the city's top-notch galleries and museums. Then, if you enjoy shopping, be sure to visit the Parnell district for some one-of-a-kind products. (Exploring the entirety of Auckland will take one day.)

Taupo. The best one-day walk you will ever take is available, as is trout fishing in Tongariro Crossing. (Exploring the entirety of Taupo will take one day.)

Wellington. Learn more about the diverse aspects of Maori culture at the New Zealand Museum, Te Papa Tongarewa. After that, you can eat dinner by the water. (Exploring the entirety of Wellington will require one day.)

South Island

Christchurch.

While traveling to Christchurch, a detour can be taken to Kaikoura, the Banks Peninsula, or Hanmer Springs. Visit the Hagley Park, the Botanic Gardens, or the International Antarctic Center. (Exploring all of Christchurch will take two days.)

Mt. Cook or Aoraki. From Christchurch, you can make a pit stop and enjoy a picnic either Lake Pukaki or Lake Tekapo. Then, see Mt. Cook's glacial lakes, which are close by. Although you might encounter some challenging circumstances, Mt. Cook National Park is worthwhile. Mountaineers or not, you may still enjoy the breathtaking scenery. The park's alpine walks, which begin close to the settlement, are another option. The trip back would take roughly three hours. By participating in tours to the Tasman Glacier, going flightseeing, or stargazing, you can make the most of your stay in Mt. Cook. (Exploring all of Mt. Cook/Aoraki will take one day.)

Queenstown. One of the regions in New Zealand where you may engage in a variety of exhilarating activities is this one. You can go river rafting, Bungee jumping, or enjoy a jet boat trip. A helicopter journey through the Remarkable mountains is an option. Additionally, you may unwind and take in Lake Wakatipu's landscape. (Exploring Queenstown in its entirety will require two days.)

Milford Sound. You can travel through Fiorland in the morning after an overnight cruise. While on the voyage, you will be in awe of New Zealand's landscape, including its mountains and lakes. The boat tours are accessible throughout the day. You can go diving, sea kayaking, or flightseeing outside for more daring pursuits. (Exploring Milford Sound in its entirety will take one day.)

Wanaka. This location in New Zealand offers both land and sea activities. The lake is the fourth largest in the United States. Mountain biking, hiking, shopping, and visiting museums are all options. You can also attend Warbirds Over Wanaka, New Zealand's largest three-day air show. If you appreciate the water, you can go cannoning, kayaking, or fishing. (Exploring Wanaka thoroughly will take two days.) Fox Glacier/Franz Josef Glacier. Enjoy the magnificence of Franz Josef's forests, icy blue rivers and pools, and flowing waterfalls.

A visit of a glacier can also be scheduled in advance. The entire Franz Josef may be explored in one day.

Hokitika.

This area once served as a major river port. Additionally, it has fascinating information about the west coast's past, including details about shipwrecks, pounamu hunters, and gold miners. Visit the glowworm grotto if you want to try something new, preferably at dusk. Observing the glowworms shine like the stars in the night sky is peaceful. You can also take a stroll through the village, drink coffee on the sand, or chisel a piece of greenstone. (Exploring the entirety of Hokitika will take one day.)

Arthur's Pass. Despite being in a rural area, this location is worth visiting because of its stunning vistas. The highest pass in the Southern Alps is allegedly located in this national park. On its eastern side, you can see broad swaths of beech forest as well as riverbeds that are covered in shingles. You will encounter thick forests and gorged rivers on the western side. Additionally, you can travel on the Tranz Alpine rail service and savor the breathtaking scenery. Before returning to Christchurch, make sure to stop at the location. (Exploring Arthur's Pass in its entirety will require one day.)

During your final two days in New Zealand, take it easy for two days. Return to Christchurch. You could go shopping if you wanted to. After that, leave Auckland for home the following day. You can still go on a few last-minute excursions while in Auckland, but you should get enough rest before your trip home to prevent missing it totally due to exhaustion.

Chapter 7:
New Zealand: People And Culture

Discovering Maori

The Maori culture of this amazing country is another reason to go there. Since they arrived in New Zealand more than a thousand years ago, the Maori are considered the country's indigenous population.

It's often said that getting to know the locals is the best way to adapt to a new place. This is especially true in New Zealand, and the best place to start is by understanding more about the Maori people who have lived there the longest.

The Maori people, New Zealand's native Polynesian population, arrived in the early to mid-1300s. The Maori culture, rich in art and history, continues to play a key role in defining New Zealand's identity even after hundreds of years.

Respect is necessary when learning about the Maori culture, as it is when discovering any other new culture when traveling. You can travel with consideration if you have some background knowledge.

The People

It wasn't until the 20th century that the Maori started to recover from the significant (unfavorable) effects of the early European immigration to New Zealand in the late 17th century. Even while they struggled for their rights in modern society, they protected and respected their culture.

Due to their reputation as a warrior people, the Maori have never been defeated by English colonists. This is something that the proud Maori people are quite proud of, and they love to brag about it.

The Maori migrated from Polynesia to New Zealand in the thirteenth century. They had set out in huge ocean-going canoes, ranging in length from twenty to forty meters, and had come in waves. They ultimately made their way to the islands, where they survived by surviving on the abundant environment.

As a result of European interaction, the Maori had internal troubles in the 17th century, which eventually led to conflict. Furthermore, illness had an impact. By the 1870s, influenza, measles, and smallpox had killed 10 to 50 percent of the Maori population. By the 19th century, the Maori population had been reduced by almost half. Relations between settlers and the Maori only started to improve until the Treaty of Waitangi was signed, a historic pact that partially restored the Maoris' sovereignty over the land.

Currently, 600,000 Maori people make up 15% of the population in New Zealand. In addition to continuing to face social and economic prejudice, Maori people also have a shorter life expectancy than the country's other ethnic groups.

Although "Maori" is frequently used, the name of the Maori language is Te Reo. Up until the 1860s, it ruled New Zealand's linguistic landscape.

The Maori would perform a " Haka " dance before a battle (which you may witness at the cultural presentation). The Maori had yet to write a written language before the arrival of the Europeans. Their forebears passed down oral tradition and history to them. Tattooing is a significant component of Maori culture. In the past, people have used tattoos to signify their status or rank.

New Zealand is home to many geothermal geysers, which are used to slowly prepare a traditional Maori food called "Hangi" underground. The entrance to the Maori gathering area requires a "Powhiri" to welcome you (or "Marae"). In addition to shouting and chanting, a warrior will confront the group. Visitors must show proof of their good faith before being allowed in.

If you're determined to learn more about the Maori. Rotorua is well-known for its educational options. A variety of cultural events and educational trips are available in the area. A Maori told me that the Bay of Islands is the finest spot to learn about the Maori. You can visit various traditional villages and take in the scenery's numerous geysers in addition to the excellent cultural acts that are given there. It is the ideal location to learn more and enjoy a performance because the area is important to Maori culture and history.

The cultural trips are equivalent in many ways (some are shorter, some have better meals, and some are of a different length), but you learn and encounter many of the same things that will have a profound impression on you. It consistently ranks among the top programs worldwide as well as in this country.

An overview of Maori history, culture, and way of life is provided throughout the program. In essence, it provides a fascinating introduction to how they have changed over time.

The cultural performances, which take place in their forest amphitheater and last around four hours, feature a normal four-course lunch, seasonal ceremonies, and other performances. There are numerous performances, and each person's ticket costs between $250 and $300 NZD. There are further options for traditional performances in Rotorua, including Mitai Maori Village. Most people concur that it has the same kind of experience and is just as pleasurable. The price of a ticket is between 129 and 135 NZD.

These places offer more than simply a cultural show because the food and music are so captivating. There is little doubt that travelers will enjoy the experience. If you want to understand Maori culture more, you should also visit the Rotorua Museum. You can learn more about the Maori people and see some interesting historical relics here. Check the schedule beforehand to see which tours and programs are still offered. If you can't make it to Rotorua, think about going to a cultural performance in Auckland or the Bay of Islands, where you can also see the site of the historic Waitangi Treaty signing between the British and Maoris.

The Museum of New Zealand Te Papa Tongarewa in Wellington is a fantastic substitute if you can't make it to Rotorua and want to learn more about Maori culture.

A trip to New Zealand is complete after studying the Maori, their history, and their culture. They bond closely with New Zealand's past, present, and future. Your understanding of them and the nation will grow in depth and insight as you learn more about them.

Marae

An exclusive hapu (sub-tribe), iwi (tribe), or whanau is the owner of a marae, a Maori gathering place (family). Usually, they have a dining room, a kitchen, a bathroom, and an open space in front of the meeting house (wharenui), carved inside and out.

Visiting one of the country's many maraes is an excellent way to immerse yourself in the culture. You should be aware of a few etiquette standards before attending these meeting areas to respect Maori customs. Maraes are venues for tribal events such as meetings, burials, festivals, educational activities, and cultural displays for tourists.

Only those who have been officially invited may enter a marae. The most frequent way for visitors to observe a marae is via taking part in a Maori "cultural experience" that is frequently provided to visitors.

Due to the increased concentration of Maori immigrants on the North Island when they first immigrated to New Zealand, there are more possibilities to participate in cultural events, especially at Rotorua.

These cultural celebrations usually feature traditional welcoming ceremonies, Maori dancing, storytelling, and a Hangi feast (meal cooked in an underground oven). Most of your visiting manners should be followed at the powhiri (welcome ceremony).

Starting The Powhiri

Now is your chance to take part in intriguing Maori traditions. Even while some powhiri components differ from tribe to tribe, the following usually happens.

Before the rite starts, a member of the iwi or whanau will greet you and take you onto the marae. They will let you know what will happen and move through customs before anything embarrassing happens.

The challenge

The following portion is still quite interesting to witness even though it is rarely carried out. It is a more typical aspect of the welcome.

A warrior will assess if the host tribe is hostile or amicable (which includes you and your squad). The All Blacks rugby team's well-known Haka is one example of chanting or dancing that might be involved. If a fighter makes faces at you, sticks out his tongue, or rolls his eyes into the back of his head, don't laugh. That is very impolite. Simply maintain a neutral expression.

The warrior will lay down a token for the tribal chief to take, which is often a branch. If traveling in a group, choose a tribe leader to take the branch to show that you are traveling in peace.

Karanga, Song, and Speech.

As you enter the marae, the host tribe's female members will start singing a karanga (a welcome call). Usually, a woman from the host tribe would answer with a song from their own

49

people. That's incredible that you can sing! If not, the iwi person who first welcomed you will give you advice.

On the grounds or within the meeting house, the host tribe and the guest tribe will sit on chairs and face one another. Taking your shoes off before walking inside the meeting place is customary. Each tribe's elder members will talk and sing. Undoubtedly, the Maori people will sing and chat in their native tongue. You and your tribe should do your utmost to repay the kindness with a song.

Hongi and Hangi

The greeting ritual is over with a hongi, an intimate gesture akin to a handshake or hug. Put your hand on the other person's shoulder and touch their forehead and nose. Do not feel obligated to touch someone's nose three times if you do not want to get married to them.

Congratulations! You are now a member of the whanau! There will be far too much food and a fantastic hangi meal.

Sacred Maori Cultural Etiquette

In Maori culture, it is improper to sit at a table. Sitting at the table is disrespectful because it is where food is prepared and consumed. Even if it isn't a table intended for such use, it is only polite to avoid sitting on them. Additionally, as pillows are designed to support the head, you can sit on them. However, it is acceptable to sit on cushions. Similarly, if someone is lying down, you shouldn't step over their head.

Learn the traditions and appropriate greetings before visiting a marae. If you are traveling with a tour group and a guide, there should be a briefing, but it always helps to be prepared. The traditional hongi, a specific and unique way to greet someone, is very important in Maori culture. Just in case you misplace what you just read. Keep in mind these crucial details:

- Please remove your shoes before entering the conference room.
- If you find someone performing a Haka in front of you amusing, keep your face expressionless and chuckle.
- Never sit on something that has food on it. It is considered impolite.
- Dinner should come after a blessing from one of your hosts.

What To Note About The Maori Culture.

The greatest method to explore Maori culture is to go to a marae

Maraes are tribal gathering places that present fantastic chances for you to interact with the local Maori population and learn about their culture and history firsthand. Speeches and performances of Maori songs and dance are just a few things you might see at a marae.

Remember that you cannot simply find a marae on a map and have a cab drop you off there. Maraes, on the other hand, can only be reached via scheduled travel. The good news is that large cities such as Northland, Auckland, Rotorua, and Canterbury provide a diverse choice of moderately priced organized excursion options.

A marae requires an invitation before you can enter.

You might be wondering, "Don't I get free access since I booked my tour to go to the Marae?" Not exactly.

The Maori must first formally greet you through a powhiri, an integral part of their culture. To start the ritual, guests are typically challenged by a Maori warrior in an act referred to as a wero. That might sound ominous, but it's not a frightening occurrence. The major goal of this ceremony, which generally involves singing and the warrior giving the guests a symbol, is to ensure everyone enters harmony.

Maori tattoos vary from one another.

Even though the methods used to apply tattoos, also known as "ta moko," have evolved from chiseling to more sophisticated needle procedures, they have always played a vital role in Mori culture. Particularly tattoos represent a person's dedication to and appreciation for their culture. The uniqueness of each tattoo is an intriguing part of the Maori tattooing culture. Since each tattoo serves as an external symbol of the wearer's particular lineage, expertise, and rank within the tribe, this is typically the case. An excellent method to deepen your studies and comprehension of Maori culture is to politely inquire about tattoos.

A significant part of Maori culture is dance.

Known for its loud physical gestures, synchronized shouting, and stomping, the Haka is a traditional battle dance performed by the Maori.

The popular Haka dance is much more than simply a way to intimidate people. Haka is frequently performed at celebrations or funerals to welcome notable guests, recognize noteworthy accomplishments, or show respect.

Maori cuisine is traditionally cooked underground.

Food is cooked in a hole in the ground using the peculiar Maori cooking technique known as hangi.

Hot stones, foil, or wire baskets are frequently used to line the pit where hangi is baked. Fish, chicken, and a few vegetables are among the food kinds that are routinely prepared using the hangi technique.

Despite the apparent simplicity of cooking with hangi, the process is time- and labor-intensive. For the Maori, hangi is a chance for people to meet for extended periods in addition to the exquisite meal it creates.

Maori's native tongue is not English.

Most New Zealanders still speak English, although Cook Islands Maori, Tuamotuan, and Tahitian have sounded like Te Reo, the language of the Mori people. Since 1987, Te Reo has been acknowledged as one of New Zealand's official languages. Interestingly, the Maori people had been passing down their history and traditions orally for many years before the advent of European colonists because they lacked a written language. They occasionally even carved character scenarios into stone and wood to provide pictures for their stories.

The Mori people do not traditionally shake hands while greeting one another.

The Maori people do not greet one another in this way, even though it may seem natural to extend your hand and try at a firm handshake when you meet a new acquaintance. Instead, they exchange verbal greetings. Try to maintain composure if you attend an event where you will be talking with Maori natives.

Instead, the hongi, a much cozier and close-up salutation, is utilized (not to be confused with the hangi cooking method). The hongi involves two people inhaling simultaneously while pressing their foreheads and noses together. It is intended to symbolize how the two spirits come together.

Greenstone is valued as a treasure in Maori culture.

The term "greenstone" refers to the literal "green stone," also referred to as pounamu by the Maori, which is primarily found in rivers in portions of southern New Zealand. Greenstone is a prized possession among the Maori and is regularly passed down from generation to generation. Tools, hooks, and spears have all been made from greenstone, which the Maori used in their creations.

Now you can buy Greenstone. Jewelry and items for home décor are the most common uses for it. The ideal souvenir to take home from your journey to New Zealand with you, your friends, and your family.

The Maori population is still very significant.

Maori make up around 15% of the population of New Zealand, although they are still very important to society. More than 600,000 people in New Zealand are of Maori heritage, making them the second-largest ethnic group in the nation, according to a 2013 census.

Although some Maori also live on the South Island, the North Island today hosts most of New Zealand's Maori population. This implies that no matter what island you visit, you will come across Maori people and have the opportunity to interact with them. When visiting a foreign country, such as New Zealand, you can become more fully immersed in the local culture by learning about the Maori way of life. As a result, when you get back home, you'll respect New Zealand more.

Best Destinations to Experience the Maori Culture

When attempting to learn about Maori culture, you could become confused by all the unfamiliar terms: Aotearoa, whanau, marae, tiki, hangi, hongi, haka, poi, but what do they all mean?

Everything makes sense once you've had a taste of Maori culture. There are several ways to educate yourself about New Zealand's indigenous culture. Whether through a concert, a tour, or a stay at a Marae, New Zealand will unquestionably quench your thirst for culture (a Maori meeting place). Undoubtedly, the Haka, or battle dance, will always be performed at Maori events. Where, though, is Maori culture to be seen in New Zealand? The Bay of Plenty, Auckland, Waikato, and Northland regions account for 60% of Maori culture. Few Maori activities are available on the South Island, but only a few.

Rotorua

There is no denying Rotorua's status as THE DESTINATION for Maori culture. This famous city is the subject of numerous Maori stories. You'll hear them while participating in one of the city's many cultural activities. Visit a Maori village, one of the geothermal parks, or a place that offers organized Maori tourism. Even a night can be spent there. Some of Rotorua's Maori cultural attractions include Tamaki Maori Village, Hell's Gate Geothermal Park, Mitai Maori Village, Te Puia, and Whakarewarewa.

Bay of Islands

Visit Waitangi, one of the most important historical places in New Zealand. A pact was forged between the Maori and the Europeans at the Waitangi Treaty Grounds. You can take in local cultural acts on-site. the Bay of Islands, waka paddling (Maori canoe) is also available.

Taiamai Tours and the Waitangi Treaty Grounds are two Maori cultural landmarks in the Bay of Islands.

Auckland.

There are numerous ways to engage with Maori culture in the City of Sails, from going to traditional dance and song events at the Auckland Museum to staying at a marae on the stunning Waiheke Island.

Auckland Museum, Te Hana, Potiki Adventures, TIME Unlimited Tours, and Hike Bike Ako Waiheke Island are just a few places in Auckland where you can learn about Maori culture.

Hokianga

You can stop at Hokianga Harbour for an overnight Marae stay en route to Spirits Bay and contemplative Cape Reinga. You can stop at Hokianga Harbour for an overnight Marae stay en route to Spirits Bay and contemplative Cape Reinga. You can also go on walking tours to see Tane Mahuta, New Zealand's largest Kauri tree, and hear about the Maori stories and legends associated with the forest.

Whanganui National Park.

You may turn your Whanganui Journey on the New Zealand Great Walks into a cultural excursion by staying at a Marae. This is a truly one-of-a-kind encounter in the heart of this pristine and historic forest.

Wellington

Wellington's Te Papa Museum is a fantastic resource for learning about Maori culture because of its many hands-on exhibitions, models, and artisanal arts and crafts. The city also provides a "Maori Treasure Tour." You can spend the night on the island of Kapiti, close by, and experience Maori hospitality and some of New Zealand's unusual flora.

Canterbury.

While seeing the Willowbank Wildlife Reserve, stop by the South Island's only Maori community. Savor a delicious Hangi lunch prepared in an "earth oven" while attending a traditional event.**Waimarama.**

Waimarama Maori Tours, based in the peaceful coastal community of Waimarama in Hawke's Bay, aims to provide visitors with the most genuine Maori cultural experience possible. Visit a historic pa site to learn more about the traditions and ancestry of the Maori people.

Hokitika

Greenstone, also known as pounamu, has a long history of discovery along the West Coast of the South Island. You may take part in a Maori ceremonial right here by chiseling your greenstone. When you get back home, you will have a souvenir that you may offer as a gift to your loved ones.

Getting a Maori tattoo

Getting a tattoo with a Maori design is another long-lasting or permanent way to experience New Zealand's Maori culture. Ta Moko, also called Maori tattoos, frequently contain a narrative. You might learn much about the Maori way of life by getting your tattoo done by a Maori artist.

Chapter 8:
Useful Māori Phrases for Local Interaction

Exploring the intricacies of a foreign culture involves more than just visiting landmarks; it necessitates a genuine understanding of its language. Language connects us to people's thoughts and emotions, fostering a profound cultural connection. The "Useful Māori Phrases for Local Interaction" chapter in this guide recognizes this, bridging the gap between travelers and the vibrant Māori culture.

Imagine strolling through local markets or engaging with artisans in their native tongue. These exchanges transcend mere transactions, becoming moments of shared humanity. Learning a few fundamental Māori phrases is the first step towards this immersive experience. These phrases, carefully curated for travelers, open doors to respectful conversations and genuine connections.

Beyond practical communication, these phrases possess a deeper significance.

Uttering "Kia ora" isn't just a greeting; it's an acknowledgment of life and well-being. "Haere mai" isn't just an invitation; it's an embrace of a new friend into your space. Each phrase carries the weight of cultural values, reflecting the Māori worldview and their relationship with the land and community.

Enriching your travel experience through Māori phrases is akin to unlocking a treasure trove of traditions.

Learning to introduce yourself with "Ko [your name] tōku ingoa" goes beyond stating your name; it encapsulates the ancestral connection and heritage you carry. Expressing gratitude with "Mihi ana" extends beyond politeness; it signifies humility and reciprocity—a profound insight into Māori ethos.

Language, as a vessel of cultural wisdom, becomes a bridge to understanding.

When you say "Tēnā koe" to someone, you're acknowledging their mana (prestige) and the essence of their being.

"E noho rā" isn't merely a farewell; it's a recognition of the moment, the people, and the shared experience. These phrases encapsulate layers of meaning that can't be fully grasped without delving into Māori culture.

As you venture through New Zealand, your interactions become a journey within a journey. Each Māori phrase you utter extends an invitation—an invitation to connect, to learn, and to honor a culture deeply rooted in the land. The guide's inclusion of these phrases isn't just a utilitarian gesture; it's an invitation to weave yourself into the rich tapestry of Māori culture, an opportunity to create moments that transcend time and place.

Chapter 9:
Stunning New Zealand Attractions

New Zealand, a mystical, gorgeous, and friendly country, provides visitors with unmatched options for exploration and adventure. The vast natural woods, mountains, beaches, glaciers, thermal zones, and coves of the rocky islands have all been adequately preserved by the culture and government, which are concerned with the environment. Traditional Maori culture coexists with modernity in New Zealand's wealthy towns, quaint villages, and vast expanses of lonely wilderness. The lovely island country is in excellent shape and has much to offer everyone.

Kaikoura, South Island

The gorgeous seaside village of Kaikoura is a favorite destination for birdwatchers, environment enthusiasts, and seafood connoisseurs. Kaikoura, located between the Seaward Kaikoura Range and the Pacific Ocean, is home to fantastic coastal treks and well-liked whale-watching cruises. Along with sperm and humpback whales, visitors may also see fur seals, dolphins, and a broad range of birds, including the magnificent albatross.

Queenstown, South Island

One of the most popular travel places in New Zealand for foreign visitors is Queenstown, known as the country's adventure capital. It is tucked between the Remarkable Mountains and the shoreline of the glittering Lake Wakatipu. Intense activities, including bungee jumping, jet boating, white water rafting, paragliding, rock climbing, mountain biking, and downhill skiing, are available to tourists in this location. They can also use the incredible system of hiking trails to explore the breathtaking alpine scenery. In addition to adventurous sports, Queenstown provides all the creature luxuries, such as top-notch hotels, spas, restaurants, galleries, and boutiques. It's also a perfect starting point for a day excursion to Central Otago, where tourists may see gold-mining towns and locations from the well-known Middle Earth scenes from the Lord of the Rings movies.

Rotorua, North Island

Rotorua is one of Earth's most geologically active places because of its position on the Great Pacific Ring of Fire. The soil has something to say right now. New Zealand's extraordinary geology is displayed through bubbling mud pools, hissing geysers, volcanic craters, and steaming thermal springs, along with the forces that most of it was created by.

Visitors can learn about the region's rich Maori history and culture while taking a walking tour of these geothermal marvels and relaxing in warm mineral springs while taking in various fascinating sights.

Adventurers will have a lot to do as well. Among the activities available are mountain biking, luging, and skydiving. Additionally, the Mt. Ruapehu ski resorts are accessible from Rotorua, where trout fishing is highly popular.

Another well-liked tourist destination is Wai-O-Tapu, home to vibrant hot springs, the famous Champagne Pool, and Lady Knox Geyser close by.

Bay of Islands

One of the most well-known holiday spots in New Zealand is the magnificent Bay of Islands, which is located three hours north of Auckland. With more than 144 islands lining the beautiful bay, it is a sanctuary for yachting and sailing.

In addition to being a popular location for sport fishing, these warm seas are also home to marlin, dolphins, whales, and penguins. Sea kayakers can explore the coastline, climb the numerous island trails, relax on tranquil beaches, travel to Cape Brett and the well-known rock formation known as the Hole in the Rock, and discover subtropical woods with Kauri trees. This gorgeous bay can be explored from the small nearby towns of Russell, Opua, Paihia, and Kerikeri.

Sky Tower

Auckland, also called the "City of Sails," has a population of over 1.6 million, making it the largest city in New Zealand and the most populous Polynesian city in the world. Auckland is fortunate to have two lovely harbors. The city is a great place to start day trips and wilderness expeditions because it is bordered by beaches with blond and black sand, hiking trails through rainforests, and stunning coves, islands, and volcanoes.

The largest city in New Zealand is home to The Sky Tower, a communications and observation tower. The Sky Tower is a well-known feature in Auckland's skyline, the largest free-standing building in the Southern Hemisphere at 328 meters (1,076 feet). The Orbit rotating restaurant atop the tower offers delectable cuisine and views that extend up to 80 kilometers away.

New Zealand's Most Beautiful National Parks

Abel Tasman National Park

It is hard to picture his thoughts when he first saw the breathtaking beach, which is why it was given his name. He was the first European to find New Zealand. The breathtakingly magnificent Abel Tasman National Park is unlike any other national park in New Zealand. Its stunning sandy beaches, crystal-clear waters, and forested interiors are all distinctive qualities.

Despite being the smallest, it packs a powerful punch thanks to its beautiful location and the abundance of people who flock there yearly. Campers can set up in the park or venturing into the forest to find one of the magnificent waterfalls that run into pools below. Kayaking is a terrific activity in the calm coastal waters, and the lovely shoreline is magnificent to view from the water.

Nelson Lakes National Park

If you want to find lovely lakes ringed by picturesque mountains, head to Nelson Lakes National Park. Because of the deep blue color, they emanate and their location in the midst of rugged valleys and ravines that give way to low-lying mountains, the two lakes of Rotoiti and Rotoroa look lovely.

You'll have plenty of chances to take amazing pictures there as the sky above them and Saint Arnaud and Mount Robert Mountain ranges are mirrored in the magnificent surroundings. From the lake's edge, paths and trails wind up the rocky mountainside and end at breathtaking lookout points with views of the picturesque panoramas below.

It is a well-liked spot for fishing due to the number of living lakes, and many tourists choose to camp and spend the night in the park's unspoiled beauty. There are many attractions to view in Nelson Lakes National Region, a serene and lovely area to visit.

Tongariro National Park

The craggy, desolate environment is so stunning — almost surreal — and is broken up by sparkling turquoise lakes. Given the stunning surroundings, it's remarkable that it was only the fourth national park ever to be established. Within the park are three active volcanoes, including Tongariro, the source of the national park's name. In the park, situated in the middle of the North Island, you can also observe lava fields and lakes that have developed in the craters of extinct volcanoes.

Mount Tongariro's snowy magnificence, as depicted in The Lord of the Rings trilogy, has made it famous around the world. The stunning natural splendor of Tongariro National Park, a Maori homeland with many sacred sites, has to be seen to be believed.

Te Urewera National Park

Entering the wildness of Te Urewera National Park is an extraordinary experience due to its untamed nature and enormous woods that spread as far as the eye can see.

The stunning Lake Waikaremoana is, without a doubt, Te Urewera's treasure. Here, breathtaking beauty is on display, and it is enthralling to see how the stillness of the lake's waters contrasts with the wild forest that threatens to encroach on its shores.

The dense forest conceals many stunning waterfalls. Lichen and moss are colonizing the rocks on both sides of the cascades. They are breathtaking in their magnificence but completely isolated from the rest of the world. Like the rest of New Zealand, this national park is beautiful. You will see things that will blow your mind, making you want to return again and again.

Arthur's Pass National Park

The mountains are painted in a stunning array of vibrant yellows and oranges as the sun sets over the national park, gradually fading into darker tones of purple as yet another lovely day comes to an end.

There are many excellent vantage points over the surrounding countryside at Arthur's Park National Park, with impressive sunsets. The Southern Alps Mountain range contains a wild area where the park is situated.

The range that cuts through the park divides it in half, with stony peaks on one side and lush forests and winding riverbeds on the other. Arthur's Pass offers a variety of exciting sports to tempt tourists, including skiing, mountaineering, and even hunting.

Best Museums in New Zealand

Tawhiti Museum

Nigel Ogle, a local artist, has dedicated his life to creating the Tawhiti Museum, which features a variety of scale and full-size dioramas and models that depict the past with extraordinary attention to detail.

The museum has a wonderful history since it was formerly a cheese factory, enhancing the fascinating experience. The museum's exhibits are divided into sections depicting various facets of life, such as railroads, farming, and shipping. The museum also offers the Tawhiti Bush Railway and Traders and Whalers experiences, which allow you to ride a railway and a boat as part of your visit. It's the best private museum in the country, fascinating and enjoyable to explore. You can drive to some fantastic spots along the North Island's west coast.

Steampunk HQ

Steampunk HQ in Oamaru is another distinctive and specialty museum in New Zealand. Although it originated in literature, the steampunk subgenre of popular culture has now spread to graphic novels and film. It is based on a sci-fi or fantasy universe in which powered machinery from the Victorian era coexists with technology, typically in a dystopian environment. The Will Smith-starring movies Mad Max, Wild Wild West, and Mortal Engines serve as good examples of this.

The ideal setting for a museum dedicated to a genre that was so profoundly impacted by the period is Steampunk HQ, a museum that celebrates all things Steampunk and is housed in a lovely old 1883 stone building in the Victorian neighborhood of Oamaru.

With sculptures, sounds, and motion pictures inspired by steampunk, the museum provides an immersive and participatory experience. A Steampunk costume booth is also there, where you can take fantastic selfies.

Waikato Museum

The museum opened its doors in a spectacular location overlooking the beautiful Waikato River in 1987. It covers various topics, including science, Tangata Whenua (Maori people), social history, and visual art. The Waikato Museum also offers 13 galleries, 25 brand-new exhibitions, and 100 public events annually. Highlights include the spectacular Maori War Canoe (Te Winika) and the Waikato WWI narrative "For us they fell."

Canterbury Museum

Planning a trip to Canterbury Museum, which opened its doors in 1867 and is housed in a spectacular historical Gothic Revival structure, is sufficient.

The museum uses a range of interactive exhibits and artifacts to illustrate the natural and cultural heritage of the Canterbury region. Rare Maori artifacts, artifacts from the earliest European settlers, displays of land and animals, and more may be found here. The Antarctic Exhibit, one of the most well-liked attractions, features a variety of expedition tales from that continent in addition to exhibits like a Tucker Sno Cat tractor from the 1950s.

The Kauri Museum

Kauri trees in the area were felled in the early years of European colonization for their wood and gum. The focus of the Kauri Museum is on this. The largest collection of kauri furniture and gum in the world and precise replicas of real sawmills, dioramas of gum diggers' huts, and other fascinating relics are all kept in the Kauri Museum. It is a lovely undiscovered hidden gem highlighting a beautiful time in local and New Zealand history.

Best Beaches in New Zealand

Every type of beachgoer can find a beach in New Zealand, from crowded urban beaches to secluded coves and famous surfing spots to island hotspots. Enjoy enormous panoramas at all of them as you soak up the sunshine on one of Auckland's top beaches, go hiking and enjoy the sun and sand at some of the nation's most remote sites near Abel Tasman National Park.

Scorching Bay Beach, Wellington

Visit Wellington's Scorching Bay Beach to soak in the sun at the farthest southern tip of the North Island. This well-liked sandbar is great for its water-based activities.

Visiting this lovely beach in Wellington, situated on the Miramar Peninsula and has a mix of grassy and sandy areas, for a picnic is one of the nicest things to do there.

Swimming will help you cool off, and snorkeling above the rocky area will allow you to see some of the many different fish species, anemones, and crayfish that might be present there. Relax with refreshments at the well-known seaside café, where they serve wonderful milkshakes and coffee.

Piha Beach

Surfers will want to head to Piha Beach since it has some of the best waves in all New Zealand. In about 45 minutes, you may leave the bustle of Auckland and arrive in a paradise of black sand beach, towering cliffs, and the azure waters of the Tasman Sea. In this nation, Malibu board riding is credited with having begun on the unspoiled sands of Piha Beach. In the 1930s, it served as the venue for the initial surf boat race in New Zealand.

Enjoy the sunshine and the breathtaking coastal scenery while watching surfers master the infamous waves.

Hikers have an exciting experience on the several hiking routes close to the beach. The protected natural area, which is situated on the outskirts of the Waitakere Ranges, contains subtropic forests.

The best way to alternate between a day at the beach and a day of hiking is to explore this area. Piha Beach is one of the must-see New Zealand beaches.

Mount Maunganui Beach

One of the nicest beaches in New Zealand's North Island is Mount Maunganui Beach, sometimes known as "The Mount" by locals.

The east coast town of Tauranga in the Bay of Plenty is home to the popular swimming and surfing spot, a stretch of white sand. The wooded Mount Maunganui frames one beach end and provides a stunning backdrop.You may get in on the action by visiting one of the many restaurants or bars directly on the sand. Crossing the harbor to Pilot Bay, where you may swim or participate in activities like stand-up paddleboarding, is one of the most exciting things to do in Tauranga.

Onetangi Beach

One of Waiheke Island's most popular beaches is 45 minutes away from Auckland's city center by ferry. Due to its stunning views of the Great Barrier and Little Barrier islands across the Hauraki Gulf, Onetangi Beach, which spans a mile and is the largest, is a tourist favorite.

Onetangi Beach, one of Auckland's prettiest beaches, is a delightful place to spend the day, whether you unwind on the sand and take in the scenery, walk to exercise, or enjoy a picnic by the water. By looking around the areas near the shore, you can discover more island experiences. Because the area is well-known for its lush hiking trails and wineries, it's easy to find something enjoyable to do.

Koekohe Beach

You can find peace at Koekohe Beach, located on the Otago coast, an hour north of Dunedin on the picturesque South Island of New Zealand. In addition to being a gorgeous beach, this one is recognized for its unique rock formations.

Moeraki Boulders, created more than 60 million years ago, are a lovely addition to the beaches at KoeKohe Beach. They are placed in a secure shore area, weighing several tons. This spot is well-liked by photographers and others interested in ancient Maori stories because the stones are supposed to be constructed of gourds and other bits of the famous canoe Araiteuru, which washed up on the shore hundreds of years ago.

Sandfly Bay

Combine a day at the beach with the chance to watch wildlife at Sandfly Bay on the Otago Peninsula. A 1.8-mile walking trail with dunes and a breathtaking coastline view leads to Sandfly Bay, one of the best sites to see birds.

Due to its resident colony of these birds, Sandfly Bay is a fantastic opportunity to observe hoiho (yellow-eyed penguins) in their natural habitat. Keep at least 150 feet away from any penguins you do manage to see to avoid startling them.

Sandfly Bay's sea lions and New Zealand fur seals may even be spotted lounging on the rocks if you're lucky. Other seabirds to watch out for are sooty shearwaters, spotted shags, and oystercatchers. The rugged beauty of Sandfly Bay, including the large dunes and coastal rock formations, makes it well worth the trip. The journey upwards is not without its rewards. Sandfly Bay is like an oyster to you. Walking along the beach, having a picnic, or playing frisbee are all enjoyable. Most Beautiful Lakes in New Zealand

Lake Pukaki

Lake Pukaki is a huge lake that abuts the Mackenzie Basin in the center of the South Island, midway between the Tasman Sea and Pacific Ocean coasts. Large lakes in the area are Lakes Tekapo and Ohau.

The lakes are surrounded by some of the most stunning alpine scenery in the nation. The lakes were produced by glaciers thousands of years ago.

Pictures of the lake's waters sometimes have a hazy, sparkling blue tinge that defies logic to occur naturally yet provides stunning visuals. Mount Cook, the area's most impressive peak, is perpetually blanketed with snow.

Emerald Lakes

The Tongariro Alpine Crossing is a full-day excursion that is one of the most popular activities for outdoor enthusiasts visiting New Zealand, including the Emerald Lakes in Tongariro National Park. The lakes have an unmistakably lunar look thanks to the magnificent volcanic rocks that surround them.

Even though the lakes get crowded during peak times, the striking color of the water in comparison to the towering mountains in the background more than makes up for it. Numerous Emerald Lakes develop various colors, such as aquamarine, jade, and turquoise, giving each one a distinctive and wonderful appearance.

Lake Rotoiti

Lake Rotoiti in New Zealand's Tasman Region is a well-liked recreation area due to its placement inside the Nelson Lakes National Park. It was known as Lake Arthur for a considerable amount of its history in honor of the English Army captain, who was one of the first Europeans to explore it in 1843.

The highest peaks of the Saint Arnaud Mountain Range encircle Lake Rotoiti, which is located high in the range.

Due to the peaks' altitude, they are perpetually covered in snow for a sizable portion of the year, giving the lake and its environs a European alpine feel that many visitors are unprepared for.

Lake Wakatipu

The largest lake in New Zealand is Lake Wakatipu, one of the country's interior finger lakes, which is around 80 km (50 miles) long and situated in the Otago Region of the South Island.

It receives its water from the Dart River in the north and is surrounded by a seductive mixture of low-lying rocky slopes that resemble desert conditions and high-altitude mountains that are frequently covered in snow.

Beaches with white sand and dedicated bathing areas are excellent places to enjoy the sun and go swimming. Boat trips are one of the most popular methods to visit the lake and offer views that aren't visible from the beach.

Lake Ohau

Lake Ohau sits on the country's South Island, in the Mackenzie Basin, which was formed centuries ago by glacier movements. It is one of three lakes with the same boundaries and a north-south location. The Hopkins and Dobson Rivers, which start their journey in the Southern Alps, supply the water for these lakes.

Lake Ohau Snow Fields is one of the best places in the country to spend winter because it offers many paths that hikers of all experience levels may use, as well as some of the highest snowfall totals in the country. Early August to early October is the typical ski season, though this can change depending on the weather. Tourists who visit during the warmer months often go fishing, hiking, or kayaking.

Lake Taupo

The same-named volcano produced the crater on the North Island of the country's Lake Taupo.

The largest lake in the nation by surface area also has year-round geysers, steam vents, and gurgling mud pools because of its volcanic history.

Seated beach sections are perfect for paddleboarders, swimmers, and sunbathers, and geothermal forces warm the lake's water in many locations. Consider going to the Mine Bay Maori carvings for an interesting cultural sight.

The thundering Huka Falls, one of New Zealand's most stunning and well-liked tourist attractions, lies near Lake Taupo.

Chapter 9:
The Top Cuisine And Beverages In New Zealand

While visiting New Zealand, there are several opportunities to sample the country's delectable cuisine and beverages. Some examples of the best food and drink in New Zealand include:

Lamb: New Zealand lamb is famous for its flavor and quality and is a popular element in many recipes. Some popular dishes featuring lamb include roast lamb with mint sauce, lamb kebabs, and lamb curry.

Seafood: New Zealand has a lengthy coastline and is recognized for its superb seafood, including fish, shellfish, and crayfish. Fish, chips, white wine-sauteed mussels, and paua (abalone) fritters are popular seafood meals.

Kiwifruit: The kiwifruit is endemic to New Zealand and is a popular and nutritious fruit. Kiwifruit can be consumed raw or prepared in a few different ways, including salad, smoothies, and sorbet.

Wine: Numerous wineries in New Zealand produce a wide variety of top-notch wines. Popular New Zealand wines include Pinot Noir from Central Otago, Riesling from the Gisborne region, and Sauvignon Blanc from Marlborough.

Beer: Numerous breweries in New Zealand produce a wide variety of delicious craft beers. The New Zealand beers Monteith's, Tui, and Speight's are a few of the most well-known.

New Zealand has many additional mouthwatering options besides the food and drink already listed. Other instances of the top cuisine and beverages in New Zealand include:

Pavlova: A meringue base is used to make the popular dessert known as pavlova, which is then topped with whipped cream and fruit in New Zealand. The pavlova, which bears the name of the Russian dancer Anna Pavlova, is thought to have originated in New Zealand or Australia.

Fush and Chups: A common snack in New Zealand is flush and chips, fish and chips battered and fried. This meal is frequently served with lemon, tartare sauce, and vinegar in coastal fish and chip joints.

Hangi: Food is cooked using the hangi, a traditional Maori cooking technique, in an underground oven. The meal is often placed in a pit lined with hot rocks and covered with earth to cook when the hangi is utilized, which happens frequently during special events.

Lamingtons: In New Zealand, squares of sponge cake covered in chocolate frosting and desiccated coconut are known as lamingtons. The Australian Governor of Queensland, Lord Lamington, is thought to have inspired the name of the Lamington.

Kumera: Kumera, also called sweet potato, is a staple ingredient in many New Zealand dishes. Some examples are kumera pie, kumera chips, and kumera and apple rosti. Kumera and other traditional Maori crops provided essential nutrition for Maori communities. The starchy and sugary kumera is now a standard in modern New Zealand cooking.

Experiencing New Zealand's rich food and beverage scene may be the highlight of your trip there. There are many delectable options to discover in New Zealand, whether you're a foodie or just seeking a nice lunch.

Traditional Maori cuisine

The regional environment and Polynesian customs have impacted traditional Maori cooking. It is a significant aspect of Maori culture. Traditional Maori food includes, for instance:

Hangi: Food is cooked using the hangi, a traditional Maori cooking technique, in an underground oven. When the hangi is used, which occurs regularly at special celebrations, the food is typically placed in a pit lined with hot rocks and covered with earth to cook.

Kumera: Kumera was a staple food for the Maori since it was grown traditionally. Kumera, a staple food often cooked in the hangi, tastes sweet and starchy.

Eel: Traditional Maori cuisine includes eel, frequently caught, and prepared in the hangi. Eel is a delectable and healthy dish loved for its luscious and soft meat.

Paua: A traditional Maori meal, paua (abalone), is frequently caught off New Zealand's rugged coasts. Paua is a delicacy frequently consumed raw or cooked on a barbeque or in a hangi.

Watercress: Watercress, a staple of traditional Maori food, is often gathered from running water. Fresh or cooked in hangi, watercress is a delicious and nutritious green.

Hāngī pīwariwari: Steamed breadfruit is transformed into Hng Pwariwari, a popular Maori specialty. Breadfruit, a starchy and nutritious fruit, is sometimes substituted for potatoes in traditional Maori cuisine.

Kāretu: The berries used to make kretu, a traditional Maori cuisine, are indigenous to New Zealand. Small and sweet Kretu berries are frequently used to make jams and jellies.

Kūmara: A traditional Maori crop, kmara, sometimes known as sweet potato, was a significant source of sustenance for Maori people. The flavor of kumara, which is sweet and starchy, is frequently cooked in the hangi.

Tītī: The nests of the sooty shearwater bird are commonly used in traditional Maori cuisine, where they are referred to as (muttonbirds). It is typically cooked on the barbecue or in a hangi.

Whaiaroaro: Fernroot is used to make the traditional Maori cuisine whaiaroaro, which is steamed in the hangi. In Maori cooking, fernroot, a starchy and wholesome vegetable, frequently takes the place of potatoes.

Traditional Maori cuisine is an important and tasty component of Maori culture, and eating it may be a highlight of any trip to New Zealand. Several Maori museums and cultural centers host traditional feasts where visitors can try various Maori dishes while learning about their history and significance.Regional specialties and local delicacies

In addition to the foods mentioned above and beverages, New Zealand also offers a wide variety of regional specialties and native cuisines. These local delicacies and regional specialties include, for instance:

Whitebait fritters: In New Zealand, whitebait, a small young fish, is used to make the meal known as "whitebait fritters." Popular at coastal fish and chip businesses, whitebait fritters are frequently paired with lemon and tartare sauce.

Pāua fritters: Paua (abalone), a delicacy in Maori cuisine, is used to make the popular New Zealand dish known as "pua fritters." Popular at coastal fish and chip businesses, pua fritters are frequently served with lemon and tartare sauce.

Fish pie: Fish, potatoes, and other vegetables are combined to make the classic New Zealand meal fish pie, which is then covered with a creamy sauce and pastry crust. A popular comfort dish on chilly and wet days is fish pie.

Kōura: In New Zealand, kura (crayfish) is a delicacy frequently caught and prepared in the many rivers and lakes of the nation. Kura is a delicious and succulent type of seafood that is sometimes served with butter and lemon.

Pavlova: With a meringue base, fruit, and whipped cream, pavlova is a beloved delicacy in New Zealand. Named after the Russian dancer Anna Pavlova, the pavlova is thought to have originated in New Zealand or Australia. One of the best parts of visiting New Zealand is trying all the delicious local cuisine. New Zealand has what you're looking for if you're into food or just looking for a delicious meal. The best places to eat and drink in New Zealand

There are many fantastic restaurants and bars in New Zealand, and there are many chances to sample regional specialties there. The following are a few instances of the top restaurants and bars in New Zealand:

Beachside fish and chip shops: Traditional fish and chip restaurants can be found in many of New Zealand's coastal towns and beaches, where you may sample mouthwatering seafood like fish, pua (abalone), and kura (crayfish). These stores have a laid-back and informal ambiance and are frequently frequented by residents and visitors.

Farmers' markets: Farmers' markets are common in New Zealand's cities and towns, where you may buy cooked goods like pies, sandwiches, cakes, and locally sourced fresh vegetables. These markets offer wonderful opportunities to sample delectable seasonal foods and help local farmers and producers.

Wineries: Numerous wineries in New Zealand produce a wide variety of top-notch wines. Numerous vineyards provide tours and tastings, and some also have eateries or cafes where you can sample regional beverages and cuisine.

Breweries: Numerous breweries in New Zealand produce a wide variety of delicious craft beers. Some of these breweries also have taprooms or pubs where you can sample their beers and other beverages. Many of these brewers also provide tours and tastings.

Maori cultural centers and museums: Traditional Maori feasts are offered by several Maori cultural institutes and museums, where you can sample a range of foods and discover their cultural significance. These feasts, frequently featuring traditional Maori dance and music performances, are a wonderful way to experience Maori food and culture.

New Zealand has many more excellent dining and drinking establishments than just those mentioned. The following are other restaurants and bars where you may enjoy New Zealand fare:

Cafes: Several excellent cafés in New Zealand serve various delectable and reasonably priced food and beverages. These eateries, which frequently provide breakfast, lunch, and snacks, are well-liked by locals and visitors.

Pubs and bars: New Zealand has a thriving pub and bar culture, and many of these places provide delectable cuisine, regional beers and wines, and a welcoming atmosphere. The live music and sporting activities that some pubs and bars host make them excellent places to unwind.

Fine dining restaurants: Several fine dining establishments in New Zealand provide top-notch fare, service, and surroundings. These eateries frequently use seasonal and local ingredients and could also specialize in a particular cuisine or culinary technique.

Street food vendors: Numerous New Zealand cities and towns have street food vendors who provide a variety of delicious and reasonably priced foods. These vendors are an excellent choice for a quick and enjoyable supper because they sell foods like burgers, hot dogs, falafel, and dumplings.

In general, New Zealand is home to many excellent eating and drinking establishments that will surely be highlights of any trip there. Many types of eateries, from those serving gourmet cuisine to those serving quick food, may be found throughout New Zealand.

Chapter 10:
Souvenirs You Must Buy in New Zealand

Natural splendor, historical significance, and cultural diversity are abundant in New Zealand. The nation provides a variety of breathtaking scenery that is likely to create a lasting effect on every traveler, from snow-capped mountains to immaculate beaches. And what better way to cherish your trip's memories than by bringing home a few trinkets that perfectly reflect this amazing place?

Here are some must-purchase trinkets in New Zealand:

1. Pounamu (Greenstone)

In New Zealand, pounamu, commonly called greenstone or jade, is revered as a sacred stone by Maori people. It's located on the South Island and is distinguished by a gorgeous shade of green. Pounamu is used to make various products, including jewelry and artistic carvings. It is frequently presented as a gift to show respect, love, and appreciation and is thought to have therapeutic abilities. You should only buy

Pounamu from a reputable vendor. Because many shops in tourist regions sell fake greenstone, it's important to find one that comes recommended by locals or has a certification of authenticity.

2. Merino Wool Products

High-quality Merino wool from New Zealand is renowned for its softness, warmth, and resilience. The nation's sheep farmers produce merino wool to make many goods, including garments, blankets, and scarves. Because they are useful, fashionable, and will serve as constant reminders of your vacation, merino wool products are wonderful souvenirs. Merino wool goods guarantee the finest quality, so look for these.

3. Manuka Honey

Manuka honey is a distinctive variety of honey made in New Zealand from the Manuka tree's nectar. It is used to treat a variety of illnesses, from sore throats to digestive problems, and is renowned for its medicinal powers.

Look for jars with a UMF (Unique Manuka Factor) rating when purchasing Manuka honey. This score serves as a gauge of the honey's quality and reveals the extent of its antibacterial activity. The honey's potency increases with the UMF rating.

4. Kiwiana Souvenirs

Kiwiana souvenirs are exclusive to New Zealand and honor its history and culture. These products might range from whimsical Kiwi-themed t-shirts and mugs to traditional Maori sculptures.

Kiwiana trinkets are excellent presents for loved ones back home since they provide a window into New Zealand's distinctive and eccentric culture. For an authentic experience, look for handcrafted or locally created goods.

5. Wine

The Marlborough region in the South Island is particularly well-known for its Sauvignon Blanc, and New Zealand has recently gained international acclaim for its wine. However, the nation also makes exceptional Pinot Noir, Chardonnay, and other varieties of wine.

You may bring a piece of New Zealand home by purchasing wine as a souvenir. Many vineyards have tours and tastings, which are a great way to sample some of the best wines in the nation while learning about the wine-making process.

6. Maori Carvings

Maori carvings are a significant component of New Zealand's cultural legacy and are frequently employed to convey narratives or spiritual meanings. These carvings are distinctive and significant keepsakes and can be seen on everything from jewelry to ornamental goods.

When purchasing Maori carvings, seek high-quality items crafted by a talented artist. Additionally, it's crucial to confirm that the carvings have been.

7. Kiwi Bird Merchandise

New Zealand's national bird and well-known symbol is the kiwi. This New Zealand-only flightless bird is renowned for its striking appearance and peculiar behavior. Since kiwi birds are nocturnal and hardly seen in the environment, purchasing souvenirs with kiwi themes is a terrific way to keep an impression of your vacation to New Zealand.

From keychains to plush animals to T-shirts, you may find a wide variety of souvenirs with Kiwi themes. Kiwi-shaped cookie cutters, Kiwi bird mugs, and Kiwi bird ornaments are a few well-liked Kiwi gifts. Additionally, you can buy items that assist the conservation of the kiwi bird to help save this threatened species.

8. All Blacks Jersey

The All Blacks, New Zealand's national rugby side, have an unrivaled reputation for being unbeatable. Many Kiwis wear their national pride on their sleeve because of the team's success on the world stage. Buying an All Blacks jersey is a great way to show your team support and makes for a stylish keepsake. In New Zealand, there are a lot of sporting goods and gift shops where you may get All Blacks shirts. The styles and sizes available include replica jerseys and customized jerseys with your name or number.

Conclusion

New Zealand has unparalleled scenery, a fascinating history, and unforgettable experiences. We hope our 2023 New Zealand Travel Guide has inspired you to plan your trip to this wonderful country.

Our guidebook is packed with carefully vetted recommendations, expert tips, and local knowledge to help you maximize your time in New Zealand. Whether you're looking to relax in a hot spring, climb a glacier, or sample the local fare, we have something for you to do.

Don't just take our word for it; book a trip to New Zealand today and experience the magic for yourself. This once-in-a-lifetime trip is waiting for you, and our expert guide will ensure you have an unforgettable experience.

The question is, "Why are you waiting?" Pack your luggage, grab a copy of our New Zealand Travel Guide 2023, and prepare for an amazing journey across one of the world's most beautiful and intriguing countries. You are most cordially invited to the land of the long white cloud.

Printed in Great Britain
by Amazon

29115686R00051